Bob Chilcott
Jussi Chydenius

Sun, Moon, Sea, and Stars

8 contemporary pieces for mixed voices

MUSIC DEPARTMENT

OXFORD
UNIVERSITY PRESS

OXFORD
UNIVERSITY PRESS

Great Clarendon Street, Oxford OX2 6DP,
United Kingdom

Oxford University Press is a department of the University of Oxford.
It furthers the University's aim of excellence in research, scholarship,
and education by publishing worldwide

Oxford is a registered trade mark of Oxford University Press
in the UK and in certain other countries

© Oxford University Press 2013

Bob Chilcott and Jussi Chydenius have asserted their rights under the Copyright,
Designs and Patents Act, 1988, to be identified as the Composers of these Works

First published 2013

All rights reserved. No part of this publication may be reproduced,
stored in a retrieval system, or transmitted, in any form or by any means,
without the prior permission in writing of Oxford University Press

Permission to perform the works in this anthology in public
(except in the course of divine worship) should normally be obtained
from a local performing right licensing organization, unless the owner
or the occupier of the premises being used already holds a licence
from such an organization. Likewise, permission to make and exploit a
recording of these works should be obtained from a local mechanical
copyright licensing organization

Enquiries concerning reproduction outside the scope of the above
should be sent to the Music Rights Department, Oxford University Press,
at music.permissions.uk@oup.com or at the address above

Impression: 1

ISBN 978-0-19-338814-7

Music origination by
Enigma Music Production Services, Amersham, Bucks.

Printed in Great Britain on acid-free paper by
Halstan & Co. Ltd, Amersham, Bucks.

Preface

We are both lucky to have sung in world-class vocal groups: The King's Singers and Rajaton. When you have sung in groups such as these—made up of six voices—the sound of interlocking vocal textures and richly coloured harmony never leaves you. Both of us have been strongly influenced by the vocal group 'sound', and we have inevitably incorporated a great deal of the rhythmic impulse and harmonic language of small-group singing into our pieces.

In this book we have tried to capture a bit of this feeling in eight new songs, designed to be sung either by a small group or by a choir. Our hope is that these songs, with opportunities for improvisation and jazz combo or band accompaniment, are flexible enough to allow groups to personalize them, while incorporating into their repertoire a little of the style and sound that has been so important to us.

Bob Chilcott and Jussi Chydenius
January 2013

Contents

Composers' Notes		5
Come back!	Bob Chilcott	6
Tonight	Jussi Chydenius	12
My Heart's Friend	Bob Chilcott	22
Deep in the night	Jussi Chydenius	30
Sun, Moon, Sea, and Stars	Bob Chilcott	41
On a Windy Day	Jussi Chydenius	52
She walks in beauty	Bob Chilcott	60
The Sound of the Sea	Jussi Chydenius	71

Composers' Notes

I have set a great deal of Native American poetry over the years, and **My Heart's Friend** is one of the most well known and personal of these. I stole the piano introduction from an arrangement of a Jimmy Webb song that I made for The King's Singers and Richard Rodney Bennett a number of years ago, and I tried to incorporate the feeling of a Jimmy Webb song into the melody line. **Come back!** sets my own words, but the inspiration came from a Seminole poem entitled 'Song for the Dying'.

I have always been a great admirer of the French musician Michel Legrand, and I particularly love his 'Once upon a summertime', to lyrics by Johnny Mercer. I tried to reflect his bittersweet style in **Sun, Moon, Sea, and Stars**, and I imagined it sung by The King's Singers. I have given a contemporary twist to the Lord Byron poem **She walks in beauty**, which includes the opportunity for a bit of vocal improvisation, and as with a few of the pieces in this collection, the accompaniment is flexible.

I have never been a musical purist, and I hope that these songs will give the opportunity for the singers to use their creativity and stylistic flair.

BOB CHILCOTT

I am a hopeless romantic and an utterly text-oriented composer. For me, composing without a touching poem is like riding a bicycle with a flat tyre—you move forward, but it's slow and certainly not fun.

On a Windy Day was the first piece I wrote for this collection, and it sets a beautiful poem by Anne Brontë. I wanted to keep the piano accompaniment simple, to match the style of the ballad, which should be performed with a wide dynamic range. **Tonight** is a love song that sounds to me as if it could appear in a French film—very romantic but a bit melancholic. Choirs should feel free to alter the scat syllables in my *a cappella* pieces. If you would rather use 'bm' than 'dm' or 'doo' than 'oo', then do it!

I was haunted by the poem **Deep in the night** by Sara Teasdale, and I felt it needed to be set to music. The downward chromatic melody in the tenors is the harmonic key to this piece, but the emphasis should be on the text and the tightness of the rhythms—make it funky but poetic. **The Sound of the Sea** is the 'biggest' of my four pieces, with piano and optional bass and drums accompaniment, and the opportunity for choirs to exploit their full dynamic range.

JUSSI CHYDENIUS

for David Lawrence and CBSO Young Voices

Come back!

Words and music by
BOB CHILCOTT
(b. 1955)

*Bars 1–4 (and all repetitions) should be played as written. Elsewhere, the piano part may be performed *ad lib.* An optional bass and drum kit part is available in PDF form as a free download from the publisher's website.

© Oxford University Press 2013. Photocopying this copyright material is ILLEGAL.

9
f
back!
Come back!
Come back, come back! Be -
T.
B. f
- fore you get to the line of the door,
11
- fore you get to the o - pen road, Be - fore you ride on the road of dreams, Be -
f
13
- fore you break my heart, come back!

16
mf
19
unis. mf
Be - fore you get to the dip in the sand,
mf
Come
21
Be - fore you get to the wa - ter's edge,
back! Come back, come back, come back!
Come

23
S. f
A.
Be - fore you get to the o - pen sea, Be -
back!
Come back, come back!
f
f
25
- fore you sail on the crest of a wave, Be - fore you break my heart, come_
27
back!

30
f
Be-
f
33
-fore you get to the break in the cloud, come back!
Come back, come back! Be-
35
-fore you get on a wing and a prayer, come back!
Come back, come back! Be-

37
- fore you get to the o - pen sky, Be - fore you fly in the face of love, Be -
39
- fore you break my heart, come back! Be -
1.
40b
2.
back!
ff
Come back!

Tonight

Sara Teasdale
(1884–1933)

JUSSI CHYDENIUS
(b. 1972)

© Oxford University Press 2013. Photocopying this copyright material is ILLEGAL.

11
gold, The sky is still, the sky
pp
oo doo doo doo doo doo doo
pp
oo doo doo doo doo doo doo
dm dm dm dm dm dm
pp
16
is still and blue; The
p
doo doo dm oo dm oo
doo doo dm dm oo dm dm oo
dm dm dm dm dm dm
p

21
moon was made for the sky, made for the
p
dm oo for the sky dm
p
dm dm oo for the sky dm dm
p
dm dm dm dm dm dm
26
sky to hold, And I for you,
3
oo sky to hold doo doo doo doo
p
oo sky to hold doo doo doo doo
dm dm dm dm dm dm

31
mp
I for you.
p
doo doo doo doo doo doo doo dm
doo doo doo doo
dm dm dm dm dm dm dm
35
mp
I for you,
doo doo doo doo doo doo doo doo doo doo doo doo
mp
I for you,
mp
dm dm dm dm dm dm dm
mp

39
mf
I for you.
doo doo doo doo doo doo doo doo doo dm
mf
I for you.
mf
dm dm dm dm dm dm dm dm
mf
43
mp
mf
The moon is a
doo doo doo doo oo doo doo doo doo oo
mp
oo The
mp
dm dm dm dm dm dm dm dm
mp

47
mp
flo - wer, a flo - wer with - out a
doo doo doo doo oo doo doo doo doo oo
mf
mp
moon is a flo - wer, a
dm dm dm dm dm dm dm dm
51
3
stem, The sky is lu - mi - nous, the
doo doo doo doo oo doo doo doo doo oo
3
flo - wer with - out a stem, The sky is
dm dm dm dm dm dm dm dm dm
3
3

55
sky is lu - mi - nous;
doo doo doo doo oo doo doo doo oo
lu - mi - nous, is lu - mi - nous;
dm dm dm dm dm dm dm dm
59
mf
E - ter - ni - ty
doo doo doo doo ah doo doo doo doo
ah
dm dm dm dm dm dm dm

62
f
mf
was made for them, e - ter - ni - ty
ah doo doo doo doo ah doo doo doo doo
f
E - ter - ni - ty was made for them,
dm dm dm dm dm dm dm dm
66
3
was made for them, To - night for
ah doo doo doo doo ah doo doo doo doo
mf
3
e - ter - ni - ty was made for them, To -
dm dm dm dm dm dm dm dm dm dm dm
3
3

70
us, to - night for us.
doo doo doo doo doo doo doo doo doo doo doo
- night for us, to - night for us.
dm dm dm dm dm dm dm
74
f
To - night for us, to -
ah doo doo doo doo To - night for us, to -
To - night for us, to -
dm dm dm dm To - night for us, to -

79
poco rall.
a tempo
p
- night for us.
- night. dm oo dm
- night. dm oo dm
- night. dm dm dm
poco rall.
a tempo
84
rit.
mp
ah
oo dm oo dm oo
oo dm oo dm dm oo
dm dm dm dm dm dm
rit.

for Tim and Natalie

My Heart's Friend

Mary Austin (abridged)
(1868–1934)

BOB CHILCOTT
(b. 1955)

© Oxford University Press 2013. Photocopying this copyright material is ILLEGAL.

SOPRANOS
10
p dolce
S.
Fair is the white star of twi - light, And the sky clear - er
13
At the day's end, the day's end;
16
mp dolce
S.
A.
She is fair-er, she is dear - er, She, my
mp dolce
T.
B.
She is fair-er, she is dear - er, She, my
mp dolce

19
mf
heart's friend. She is fair-er, she is dear - er,
mf
heart's, my heart's friend. She is fair-er, she is dear - er,
mf
my heart's friend, my heart's friend.
p
22
dim.
p
She, my heart's, my heart's friend.
dim.
p
dim.
p
26

29
TENORS & BASSES unis. p dolce
T./B.
Fair_ is the white star of
p sost.
32
pp
S.
A.
White___ star, And the moon_
T./B.
T.
twi - light,___
B.
And the moon rov - ing___ To the sky's___
35
rov - ing To the sky's___ end;
end, the sky's___ end;___

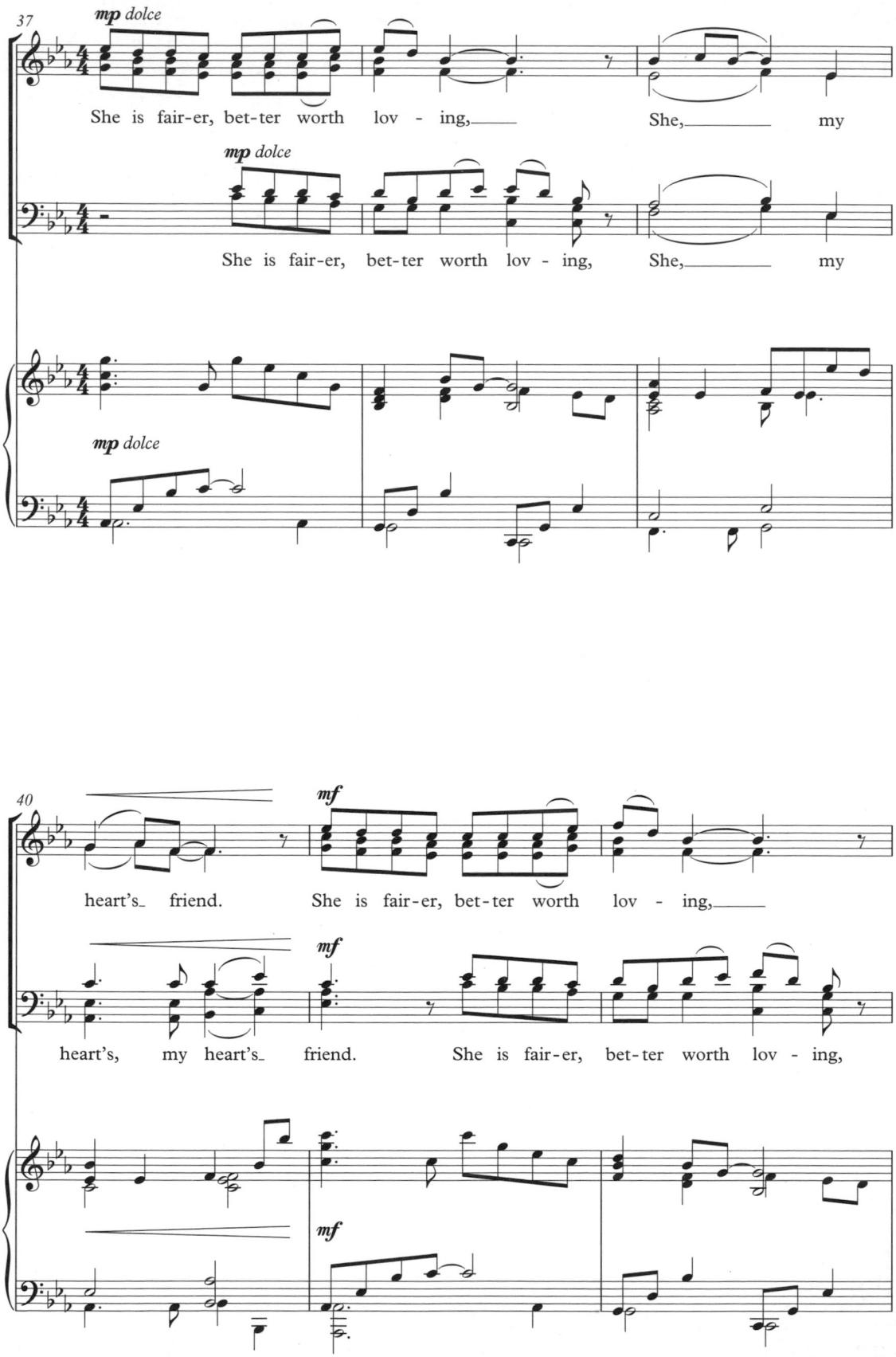
37
mp dolce
She is fair-er, bet-ter worth lov - ing, She, my
mp dolce
She is fair-er, bet-ter worth lov - ing, She, my
mp dolce
40
mf
heart's friend. She is fair-er, bet-ter worth lov - ing,
mf
heart's, my heart's friend. She is fair-er, bet-ter worth lov - ing,
mf

43
my heart's friend,
She, my heart's, my heart's friend, my heart's

46
risoluto
She is fair-er, bet-ter worth lov - ing,
friend.
risoluto
She is fair-er, bet-ter worth lov - ing,
risoluto

49
f
She, my heart's friend. She is fair-er, bet-ter worth
f
She, my heart's, my heart's friend. She is fair-er,
f

52
dim.
my heart's friend,
lov - ing,
She, my heart's, my heart's
bet-ter worth lov - ing,
dim.
dim.

55
my heart's friend.
p
friend.
p
p
p
58
rit.
My heart's friend.
rit.

Deep in the night

Sara Teasdale
(1884–1933)

JUSSI CHYDENIUS
(b. 1972)

© Oxford University Press 2013. Photocopying this copyright material is ILLEGAL.

*Keyboard reduction for rehearsal only.

24
mf
A.
Deep in the night the cry of a swal-low, un-der the stars he flew,
mf
T.
Deep in the night the cry of a swal-low, un-der the stars he flew,
mf
B.
deep in the night, deep in the night, deep in the night,
mf
27
keen as pain was his call to fol-low
keen as pain was his call to fol-low
deep in the night, deep in the night, deep in the night,

30
o - ver the world to you. Love in my heart is a
o - ver the world to you. Love in my heart is a
deep in the night, deep in the night, deep in the night,
33
cry for - ev - er lost as the swal - low's flight, seek-
cry for - ev - er lost as the swal - low's flight, seek-
deep in the night, deep in the night, deep in the night,

36
- ing for you and ne - ver, ne - ver stilled by the stars at
- ing for you and ne - ver, ne - ver stilled by the stars at
deep in the night, deep in the night.
39
night.
night.
p
Deep in the night, deep in the night, deep in the night,
p

42
S.
A.
T.
B.
p
mf
oo
deep in the night, deep in the night, deep in the night, deep in the night,
46
pp
Deep in the night the cry of a swal-low,
Deep in the night the cry of a swal-low,
Deep in the night the cry of a swal-low,
mp
deep in the night.

49
un-der the stars he flew, keen as pain was his
un-der the stars he flew, keen as pain was his
un-der the stars he flew, keen as pain was his
pp
Un-der the stars he flew,
52
call to fol-low o-ver the world to you.
call to fol-low o-ver the world to you.
call to fol-low o-ver the world to you.
Deep in the night,

55
mf
Love in my heart is a cry for-ev-er lost as the swal-low's flight,
mf
Love in my heart is a cry for-ev-er lost as the swal-low's flight,
mf
Love in my heart is a cry for-ev-er lost as the swal-low's flight,
mf
deep in the night, deep in the night, deep in the night,
mf
58
seek-ing for you and ne-ver, ne-ver
seek-ing for you and ne-ver, ne-ver
seek-ing for you and ne-ver, ne-ver
deep in the night, deep in the night, deep in the night,

61
S.
stilled by the stars at
A. 1
stilled by the stars at night,
A. 2
stilled by the stars at night,
T.
stilled by the stars at night,
B.
deep in the night, deep in the night,
64
night,
stilled by the stars at night,
stilled by the stars at night, stilled by the stars at
stilled by the stars at night,
deep in the night, deep in the night, deep in the night,

67
stagger breathing
stilled by the stars at night,
stilled by the stars at night,
stilled by the stars at night,
stilled by the stars at night,
deep in the night, deep in the night, deep in the night,
70
mp
f
mp
night,
night,
f
mp
stilled by the stars at night,
night,
f
mp
stilled by the stars at night,
night,
mp
deep in the night,
mp

74
S.
p
night.
A.
night,
T.
night,
B.
deep in the night, deep in the night, deep in the night,
77
poco rit.
p
mp
night,
night.
p
mp
night,
night.
p
deep in the night, deep in the night, night.
poco rit.
p

for Kate

Sun, Moon, Sea, and Stars

Words and music by
BOB CHILCOTT
(b. 1955)

Gentle but with rhythmic impulse ♩ = *c.*69

SOPRANO
ALTO

pp

oo *oo*

TENOR 1
†TENOR 2

pp

oo *oo*

BASS

pp

oo *oo*

Gentle but with rhythmic impulse ♩ = *c.*69

for rehearsal only

pp

4

SOLO BARITONE

p

You and I will touch the sun and

S.
A.

T. 1
T. 2

oo

B.

oo

*The keyboard reduction does not include the solo baritone part. †Alternatively, this part may be sung by Bass 1.

© Oxford University Press 2013. Photocopying this copyright material is ILLEGAL.

6
hold it in our hand. You and I will pierce the sky like
oo
oo
oo
8
mp
rain - drops in the sand. And when the sun - light shows its face it's
p
when the sun - light
p
when the sun - light
p
sun - - light
p

10
on - ly plain to see you're sun, moon, sea, and stars to me.
face, you're sun, moon, sea, and
shows its face, moon,
face, sun, moon,
shows its face, sun, moon,
shows its face, sun, moon, to
12
You and I will reach the moon and
stars, and stars.
stars to me.
oo
oo
stars.
stars to me.
oo
me.
oo

14
keep it in our sight. You and I will gent - ly fly like
Will gent - ly fly, will
You and I, oo
You and I, oo
oo
oo
16
moon- beams in the night. And when the moon - light shows its face it's
mp
gent - ly fly, when the moon - light
gent - ly fly,
mp
when the moon - light
mp
moon - - light
mp

18
on - ly plain to see you're sun, moon, sea, and stars to me.
face, you're sun, moon, stars.
shows its face, stars.
face, sun, stars.
shows its face, stars.
shows its face, sun, stars.
20
mf
You and I will
p
mp
oo
You and I will
p
mp
You and I,
oo
You and I will
p
mp
oo
You and I will
p
mp

23
sail the o - cean wide. You and I will
sail the o - cean. You and I will
the o - cean wide. You and I,
sail the o - cean wide. You and I will
sail the o - cean. You and I will
25
f
wan - der with the tide. And as the waves go roll - ing by for -
mf
wan - der with the tide. ah
with the tide. ah
mf
wan - der with the tide. ah
mf
wan - der with the tide. ah
mf

27
- ev - er you will be like sun, moon, sea, and stars to me,
sun, moon, stars to
sun, moon, stars to
sun, moon, stars to
poco rit.
a tempo
mp
29
to me.
me.
me, to me.
me.
me.
pp
oo
pp
oo
pp
oo
poco rit.
a tempo
pp

31
oo
oo
oo
oo
34
p
You and I will catch a star and cra - dle it with love.
oo
oo
oo

36
mp
You and I will see it shine for - ev - er up a - bove. And
oo
38
with the star - light look - ing down it's on - ly plain to see you're
down, you're
mp
with the star - light look - ing down,
down,
mp
with the star - light look - ing down,
mp
star - - light look - ing down,
mp

40
poco rit.
sun, moon, sea, and stars to me.
sun, moon, stars.
p
stars. oo And
sun, stars.
p
stars. oo And
p
sun, stars. oo And
poco rit.
p
42
a little slower and freer
p
You're
with the star - light look - ing down it's on - ly plain to see,
with the star - light look - ing down it's on - ly plain to see,
with the star - light look - ing down it's on - ly plain to see,
a little slower and freer

poco rit.
44
sun, moon, sea, and stars to me..
sun, moon, sea, and stars.
sun, moon, stars.
sun, moon, stars.
sun, moon, stars.
sun, moon, stars.
poco rit.
46
slower
rit.
pp
oo
pp
oo
pp
oo
pp
oo
slower
rit.
pp

On a Windy Day

Anne Brontë
(1820–49)

JUSSI CHYDENIUS
(b. 1972)

An optional bass and drum kit part is available in PDF form as a free download from the publisher's website.

© Oxford University Press 2013. Photocopying this copyright material is ILLEGAL.

9
unis. p
My soul is a - wa - kened,
pp
13
S./A.
my spi-rit is soar-ing and car-ried a-loft on the wings of the
17
breeze, and car-ried a-loft on the wings of the

21
S./A.
S.
A.
p
breeze; for a-bove and a - round me
T.
B.
p
25
the wild wind is roar - ing, a - rous - ing to rap-ture the
28
earth and the seas, a - rous - ing to rap-ture the

32
f
earth and the seas. The long with-ered grass
mf
f
The
LH
f
mf legato
36
in the sun-shine is glanc - ing, the
long with-ered grass in the sun-shine is glanc - ing,
sim.
39
bare trees are toss - ing their branch - es on high;
f

42
the dead leaves be - neath them are
45
mer - ri - ly danc - ing, the white clouds are scud - ding a -
48
- cross the blue sky, a - cross the blue sky.
p
mp

52
pp
pp
p
57
Fine
Fine
SOPRANOS & ALTOS
61
unis. p
S./A.
I wish I could see how the o-cean is lash-ing the
pp

65
S./A.
foam of its bil-lows to whirl - winds of spray,
the
unis.
T./B.
p
69
foam of its bil-lows to whirl - winds of spray;
73
S.
A.
pp
I wish I could see how its proud waves are
T.
B.
pp
Ped.

76
mp
dash - ing, and hear the wild roar of their thun - der to -
mp
mp
79
- day, and hear the wild roar of their
82
f
Repeat al Fine
thun - der to - day! The
f
Repeat al Fine
f

for Bruce Rogers and Mt. San Antonio College Singcopation

She walks in beauty

Lord Byron
(1788–1824)

BOB CHILCOTT
(b. 1955)

*The piano part may be performed *ad lib.* An optional bass and drum kit part is available in PDF form as a free download from the publisher's website.

© Oxford University Press 2013. Photocopying this copyright material is ILLEGAL.

9
And all that's best of dark and bright
11
Meet in her as - pect and her eyes:
13
p
Thus mel-lowed to that ten - der light Which
p
p

15
heav'n to gau-dy day de-nies.
She walks in
17
pp
S.
A.
beau-ty,
she walks in beau-ty,
T.
B.
pp
pp
20
oo
unis. p
One shade the more,
p

22
She walks in beau - ty,
mm
one ray the less,
Had half im-paired the name-less grace
24
oo
Which waves in ev - 'ry
26
she walks in beau - ty,
mm
ra - ven tress,
Or soft - ly light - ens o'er her face;

28
Where thoughts se - rene - ly
mp
p
oo
T.
B. p
mp
30
sweet ex - press
How pure, how dear their dwell - ing
mp
How pure, how dear their dwell - ing
mp
32
p
She walks in beau - ty,
mm
place.
p
She walks in beau - ty,
p

34
she walks in beau - ty.
she walks in beau - ty.
36
unis. p
And on that cheek, and o'er that
38
T./B.
brow, So soft, so calm, yet e - lo - quent,

40
S.
A.
mp
The smiles that win, the
T./B.
T.
B.
mp
mp
42
tints that glow, But tell of days in good-ness
44
spent, A mind at peace with

46
all be - low,
mf
A heart whose love is
mf
mf
48
in - no - cent,
in - no - cent,
in - no - cent.
She walks in beau - ty,
50
p
in - no - cent.
p
She walks in beau - ty,
She walks in beau - ty,
p
p
She walks in
p

*This repeat can be taken any number of times, at the performers' discretion. The vocal lines can be embellished *ad lib.* or sung as written.

†Diminuendo last time only.

60
she walks in beau - ty, walks in
she walks in beau - ty, walks in beau - ty, in
mm she walks in beau-ty, walks in
walks in beau - ty, she walks in beau - ty,
62
rit.
slower
beau - ty, she walks in beau - ty.
beau - ty, she walks in beau - ty.
beau - ty, she walks in beau - ty.
she walks in beau - ty.
rit.
slower

The Sound of the Sea

Henry Wadsworth Longfellow
(1807–82)

JUSSI CHYDENIUS
(b. 1972)

An optional bass and drum kit part is available in PDF form as a free download from the publisher's website.

© Oxford University Press 2013. Photocopying this copyright material is ILLEGAL.

13
S.
A.
round the peb - bly beach - es far and
T.
B.
mf
17
p
mp
wide, far and wide I
p
p
21
heard the first wave of the ris - ing tide Rush
mp
I heard the first wave of the ris - ing tide
mp

25
on - ward with un - in - ter - rupt - ed sweep.
rush on - ward with un - in - ter - rupt - ed sweep.
29
mf
p
So comes to us at times, from the un-known And
mf
mf
p
32
mf
in ac - ces - si-ble so-li-tudes of be - ing,
mf
in-ac - ces - si-ble so-li-tudes The rush-ing of the sea-
mf

36
p
mf
sea - tides of the soul;
- tides of the soul;
39
p
And in - spi-ra - tions, that we deem our own, Are some di-vine fore -
f
fore -
42
- shad-ow - ing Of things be-yond our rea - son or con -
- shad-ow ing and fore - see - ing

46
- trol.
rea - son or con - trol.
mf
51
mf
A voice out of the si -
mf
55
mp
- lence of the deep, the deep,
mp
mp

59
pp
A sound mys - te - ri - ous -
pp
pp
63
mf
p
- ly mul - ti - plied, mul - ti - plied
mf
p
p
67
mf
As of a ca-ta-ract from the moun-tain's
mf
As of a ca-ta-ract from the
mf

71
side, Or roar of winds up - on a
moun - tain's side, Or roar of winds up - on a
75
f
p
wood - ed steep. So comes to us at times,
f
wood - ed steep.
f
p
78
mf
from the un - known And in - ac - ces - si - ble so - li - tudes of
mf
in - ac - ces - si - ble so - li - tudes
mf

81
p
mf
be - ing,
sea - tides of the
The rush - ing of the sea - tides of the soul;
85
p
soul;
And in - spi-ra - tions, that we deem our own, Are
p
And in - spi-ra - tions, that we deem our own, Are
p
88
f
some di - vine fore - shad - ow - ing
Of things be - yond our
f
some di - vine fore - shad - ow - ing and fore - see - ing
f

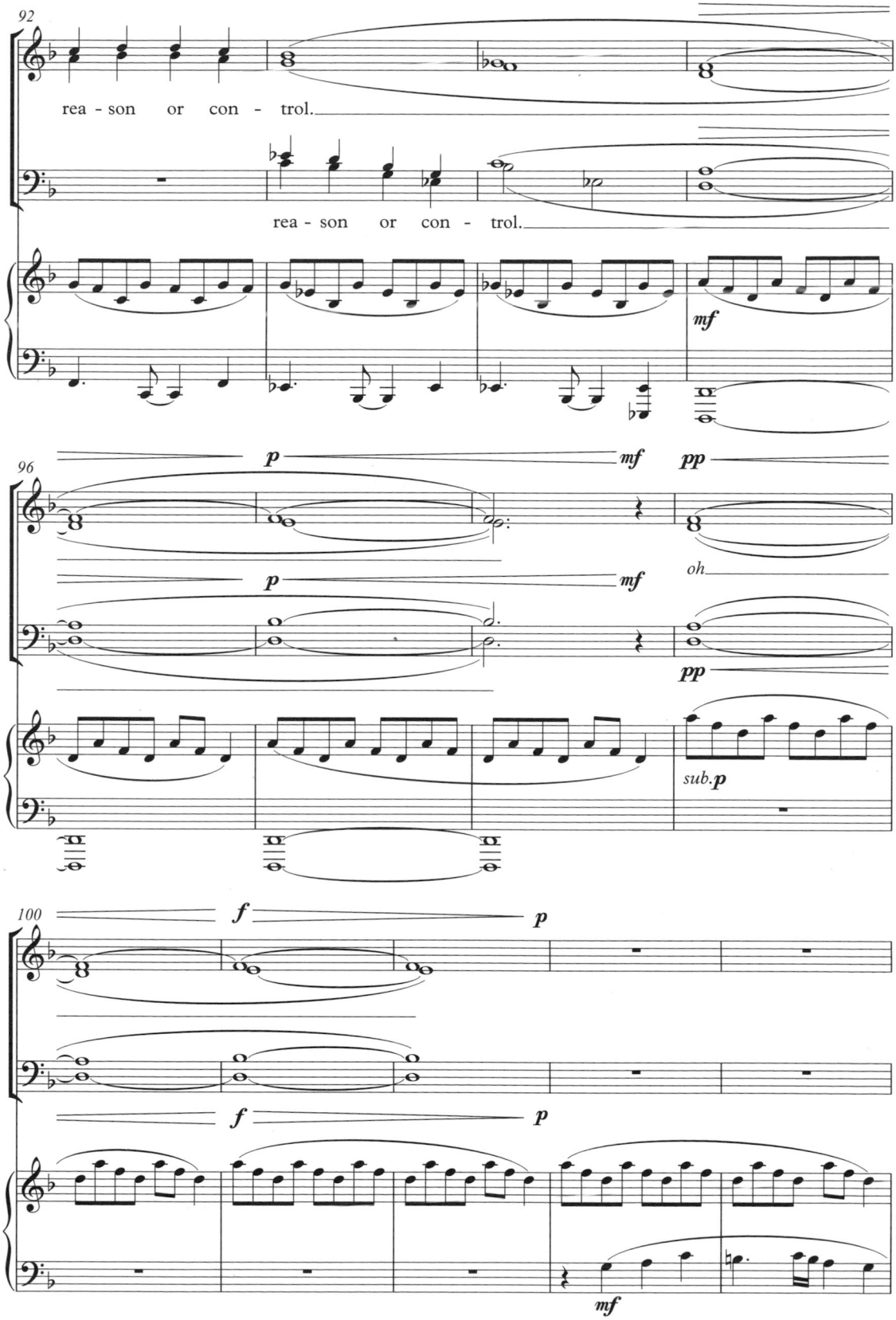
92
rea - son or con - trol.
rea - son or con - trol.
mf
96
p
mf
pp
p
mf
oh
pp
sub.p
100
f
p
f
p
mf

105
unis. mp
The sea a-woke at
unis.
mp
mp
109
mid - night from its sleep,
rall.
113
p
S.
pp
mp
A.
sleep,
sleep.
T.
B.
p
pp
mp
rall.
p
mp